ALL THE

MARVELOUS EARTH

If you have no relationship with nature you have no relationship with man. Nature is the meadows, the groves, the rivers, all the marvelous earth, the trees, and the beauty of the earth. If we have no relationship with that, we shall have no relationship with each other.

ALL THE

MARVELOUS EARTH

J Krishnamurti

Co-editors: Evelyne Blau and Mark Edwards

Produced by Still Pictures Moving Words

Designed by Mike Kenny, Bailey and Kenny, London

First edition

Published by Krishnamurti Publications of America, P.O. Box 1560, Ojai, CA 93024, USA

Printed in China by Everbest Printing Co. through Four Color Imports, Ltd., Louisville, Kentucky, USA

Krishnamurti, J. (Jiddu), 1895 – 1986
    All the marvelous earth / J. Krishnamurti ; editors, Evelyne Blau and Mark Edwards. – 1st ed.
    p. cm.
    ISBN: 1-888004-21-5 (hbk.)
    ISBN: 1-888004-22-3 (pbk.)
    1. Philosophy of nature. 2. Life. I. Title.
B5134.K75.A45 2000   299.934
          QB199-500478

Library of Congress Catalogue Card Number 99 96304

For information about Foundations, Schools, and Study Centers, please contact:

Krishnamurti Foundation of America
P.O. Box 1560, Ojai, CA 93024, USA
E-mail: kfa@kfa.org
Website: http://www.kfa.org

or,

Krishnamurti Foundation Trust Ltd.
Brockwood Park
Bramdean, Hampshire, SO24 0LQ, England
E-mail: kft@brockwood.org.uk
Website: http://www.brockwood.org.uk/kft/

HarperCollins Publishers, Inc., have generously given permission to use quotations from the following works of J. Krishnamurti: Pages 11, 19, 31, 84, from *Krishnamurti to Himself*, Copyright 1987; Pages 15, 16, 20, 24, 32, 47, 51, 55, 56, 59, 64, 72, 92, from *The Only Revolution*, Copyright 1970; Pages 36, 39, from *Letters to the Schools*, Vol. 2, Copyright 1985; Page 95, from *The Awakening of Intelligence*, Copyright 1973; Page 96, from *Freedom from the Known*, Copyright 1969. *Pud Lib. 6.13.06 (2)*

The following quotations have been reprinted by arrangement with the Krishnamurti Foundation Trust Ltd.: Pages 12, 27, 40, 44, 63, 68, 71, 76, 80, 83, 99, 100, 102, from *Krishnamurti's Notebook*, Copyright 1976; Pages 67, 79, from *Meditations*, Copyright 1979; Page 23, from *Meeting Life*, Copyright 1991; Pages 28, 48, 60, from *Krishnamurti's Journal*, Copyright 1982; Pages 2, 87, from an unpublished talk at Mumbai, India, January 1982; Page 8, from *On Nature and the Environment*, Copyright 1991; Page 105, from an unpublished talk at Chennai, India, December 1979.

Introduction

The last 50 years has witnessed a period of unprecedented environmental destruction. This book acknowledges our problems but focuses primarily on all the marvelous earth.

The text is drawn from a lifetime's passionate observation of nature by the 20th-century philosopher J. Krishnamurti. In his many books and talks on the human condition he would frequently preface or incorporate observations of the world of nature into the body of his work.

These exquisitely written passages are not merely an introduction to his philosophic writings, but can be seen as the very wellspring of his most profound concerns. Krishnamurti stands alone in his acute powers of perception and sensitivity to nature and human nature. His passionate insistence that we see the totality of life with clear eyes resonates through these pages.

Our perception is not only with the eyes, with the senses, but also with the mind, and obviously the mind is heavily conditioned. So intellectual perception is only partial perception, yet perceiving with the intellect seems to satisfy most of us, and we think we understand. A fragmentary understanding is the most dangerous and destructive thing.

The pictures in this book are drawn from a large archive of photographs that illustrates both nature and our environmental problems. Krishnamurti traveled widely during the course of his annual talks in various countries. These pictures represent a diversity of his observations. They seek to illuminate rather than document the actual locations described in the text.

The editors have been deeply affected by Krishnamurti's connection to the world of nature, and hope that the juxtaposition of pictures with these writings will serve to introduce this crucial message to those who are concerned with order within ourselves, our relationship with others, and our rightful place in the world of nature.

Mark Edwards   Evelyne Blau
January 2000

…what is beauty? This is one of the most fundamental questions, it is not superficial, so don't brush it aside. To understand what beauty is, to have that sense of goodness which comes when the mind and heart are in communion with something lovely without any hindrance so that one feels completely at ease— surely, this has great significance in life; and until we know this response to beauty our lives will be very shallow. One may be surrounded by great beauty, by mountains and fields and rivers, but unless one is alive to it all one might just as well be dead.

Have you any relationship with nature, with the birds, with the water of that river? All rivers are holy, but getting more and more polluted: you may call it Ganga, or the Thames, the Nile, the Rhine, the Mississippi, or the Volga. What is your relationship with all that— with the trees, with the birds, with all the living things that we call nature? Aren't we part of all that? So, aren't we the environment?

There is a tree by the river and we have been watching it day after day for several weeks when the sun is about to rise. As the sun rises slowly over the horizon, over the trees, this particular tree becomes all of a sudden golden. All the leaves are bright with life, and as you watch them as the hours pass by, that tree whose name does not matter— what matters is that beautiful tree—an extraordinary quality seems to spread all over the land, over the river. And as the sun rises a little higher the leaves begin to flutter, to dance. And each hour seems to give to that tree a different quality. Before the sun rises it has a somber feeling, quiet, far away, full of dignity. And as the day begins, the leaves with the light on them dance and give it that peculiar feeling that one has of great beauty. By midday its shadow has deepened and you can sit there protected from the sun, never feeling lonely, with the tree as your companion. As you sit there, there is a relationship of deep abiding security and a freedom that only trees can know.

Towards the evening when the western skies are lit up by the setting sun, the tree gradually becomes somber, dark, closing in on itself. The sky has become red, yellow, green, but the tree remains quiet, hidden, and is resting for the night.

If you establish a relationship with it, then you have relationship with mankind. You are responsible then for that tree and for the trees of the world. But if you have no relationship with the living things on this earth, you may lose whatever relationship you have with humanity, with human beings.

There was a patch of blue sky between two vast, endless clouds; it was a clear, startling blue, so soft and penetrating. It would be swallowed up in a few minutes and it would disappear for ever. No sky of that blue would ever be seen again.

It was snowing that morning. A bitter wind was blowing, and the movement upon the trees was a cry for spring. In that light, the trunks of the large beech and the elm had that peculiar quality of grey-green that one finds in old woods where the earth is soft and covered with autumn leaves. Walking among them you had the feeling of the wood—not of the separate individual trees with their particular shapes and forms—but rather of the entire quality of all the trees.

The other day, as we went up the deep canyon which lay in shadow with the arid mountains on both sides, it was full of birds, insects, and the quiet activity of small animals. You walked up and up the gentle slope to a great height, and from there you watched all the surrounding hills and mountains with the light of the setting sun upon them. It looked as though they were lit from within, never to be put out. But as you watched, the light faded, and in the west the evening star became brighter and brighter. It was a lovely evening, and somehow you felt that the whole universe was there beside you, and a strange quietness surrounded you.

As you sat quietly without movement, a bobcat, a lynx, came down. As the wind was blowing up the valley it was not aware of the smell of that human being. It was purring, rubbing itself against a rock, its small tail up, and enjoying the marvel of the earth. Then it disappeared down the hill among the bushes. It was protecting its lair, its cave or its sleeping place. It was protecting what it needs, protecting its own kittens, and watching for danger. It was afraid of man more than anything else, man who believes in God, man who prays, the man of wealth with his gun, with his casual killing. You could almost smell that bobcat as it passed by you. You were so motionless, so utterly still that it never even looked at you; you were part of that rock, part of the environment.

There is a peculiar silence when it rains, and that morning in the valley all the noises seemed to have stopped—the noises of the farm, the tractor, and the chopping of wood. There was only the dripping from the roof, and the gutters were gurgling.

It was quite extraordinary to feel the rain on one, to get wet to the skin, and to feel the earth and the trees receive the rain with great delight; for it hadn't rained for some time, and now the little cracks in the earth were closing up. The noises of the many birds were made still by the rain; the clouds were coming in from the east, dark, heavily laden, and were being drawn towards the west; the hills were being carried by them, and the smell of the earth was spreading into every corner. All day it rained.

Beauty is dangerous. Standing on that hill, one saw 300 miles of Himalayas, almost from horizon to horizon, with deep, dark valleys, peak after peak with everlasting snow, not a house in sight, not a village, not a hut. The sun was touching the highest peaks, and all of a sudden the whole continuous range was afire. It was as though they were afire from within, a glow of incredible intensity. The valleys became darker and the silence was absolute. The earth was breathless in its splendour. As the sun rose from out of the far east, the immensity, the utter purity of those majestic mountains seemed so close one could almost touch them, but they were many hundreds of miles away.

And the day began.

The river that morning had a strange movement of its own; it didn't seem to be ruffled by the wind, it seemed almost motionless and had that timeless quality which all waters seem to have. How beautiful it was! No wonder people have made it into a sacred river. You could sit there, on that veranda, and meditatively watch it endlessly. You weren't day-dreaming; your thoughts weren't in any direction—they were simply absent.

And as you watched the light on that river, somehow you seemed to lose yourself, and as you closed your eyes there was a penetration into a void that was full of blessing. This was bliss.

Dawn was slow in coming; the stars were still brilliant and the trees were still withdrawn; no bird was calling, not even the small owls that rattled through the night from tree to tree. It was strangely quiet except for the roar of the sea. There was that smell of many flowers, rotting leaves and damp ground; the air was very, very still and the smell was everywhere. The earth was waiting for the dawn and the coming day; there was expectation, patience, and a strange stillness.

It is not that extraordinary blue of the Mediterranean; the Pacific has an ethereal blue, especially when there is a gentle breeze from the west as you drive north along the coast road. It is so tender, dazzling, clear and full of mirth. Occasionally, you would see whales blowing on their way north and, rarely, their enormous head as they threw themselves out of the water. There was a whole pod of them blowing; they must be very powerful animals. That day the sea was a lake, still and utterly quiet, without a single wave; there was not that clear dancing blue. The sea was asleep and you watched it with wonder.

Man has killed millions of whales and is still killing them. All that we derive from their slaughter can be had through other means. But apparently man loves to kill things: the fleeting deer, the marvelous gazelle, and the great elephant. We love to kill each other. This killing of other human beings has never stopped throughout the history of man's life on this earth. If we could, and we must, establish a deep, long abiding relationship with nature—with the actual trees, the bushes, the flowers, the grass, and the fast moving clouds—then we would never slaughter another human being for any reason whatsoever.

It was a lovely morning with fleeting clouds and a clear blue sky. It had rained, and the air was clean. Every leaf was new and the dreary winter was over; each leaf knew, in the sparkling sunshine, that it had no relation to last year's spring.

…There were children playing about, but they never looked at that lovely spring day. They had no need to look, for they *were* the spring. Their laughter and their play were part of the tree, the leaf, and the flower. You felt this, you didn't imagine it. It was as though the leaves and the flowers were taking part in the laughter, in the shouting, and in the balloon that went by. Every blade of grass, and the yellow dandelion, and the tender leaf that was so vulnerable, all were part of the children, and the children were part of the whole earth. The dividing line between man and nature disappeared, but the man on the race-course in his car and the woman returning from market were unaware of this. Probably they never even looked at the sky, at the trembling leaf, the white lilac. They were carrying their problems in their hearts, and the heart never looked at the children or at the brightening spring day. The pity of it was that they bred these children and the children would soon become the man on the race-course and the woman returning from the market; and the world would be dark again. Therein lay the unending sorrow. The love on that leaf would be blown away with the coming autumn.

We are always using nature, either as an escape or for utilitarian ends—
we never actually stop and love the earth or the things of the earth. We
never enjoy the rich fields, though we utilize them to feed and clothe
ourselves. We never like to till the earth with our hands—we are ashamed
to work with our hands. There is an extraordinary thing that takes place
when you work the earth with your hands. But this work is done only by
the lower castes; we upper classes are much too important, apparently, to
use our own hands! So we have lost our relationship with nature.

If you hurt nature you are hurting yourself.

What is nature? There is a great deal of talk and endeavor to protect nature, the animals, the birds, the whales and dolphins, to clean the polluted rivers, the lakes, the green fields, and so on. Nature is not put together by thought, as religion is, as belief is. Nature is the tiger, that extraordinary animal with its energy, its great sense of power. Nature is the solitary tree in the field, the meadows, and the grove; it is that squirrel shyly hiding behind a bough. Nature is the ant and the bee and all the living things of the earth.

The dark pines never seemed to move, unlike those aspens which were ready to tremble at the slightest whisper. There was a strong breeze from the west, sweeping through the valley. The rocks were so alive that they seemed to run after the clouds, and the clouds clung to them, taking the shape and the curve of the rocks; they flowed around them and it was difficult to separate the rocks from the clouds. And the trees were walking with the clouds.

Have you ever noticed a tree standing naked against the sky, how beautiful it is? All its branches are outlined, and in its nakedness there is a poem, there is a song. Every leaf is gone and it is waiting for the spring. When the spring comes it again fills the tree with the music of many leaves, which in due season fall and are blown away. And that is the way of life.

It was cool in the wood, with a shouting stream a few feet below; the pines shot up to the skies, without ever bending to look at the earth. It was splendid there with black squirrels eating tree mushrooms and chasing each other up and down the trees in narrow spirals; there was a robin that bobbed up and down, or what looked like a robin.

It was cool and quiet there, except for the stream with its cold mountain waters. And there it was—love, creation, and destruction—not a symbol, not in thought and feeling, but an actual reality.

The whole horizon seemed to be filled with these clouds, range after range, piling up against the hills in the most fantastic shapes, castles such as man had never built. There were deep chasms and towering peaks. All these clouds were alight with a dark red glow and a few of them seemed to be afire, not by the sun, but within themselves.

These clouds didn't make the space; they were *in* the space, which seemed to stretch infinitely, from eternity to eternity.

A blackbird was singing in a bush close by, and that was the everlasting blessing.

There is a single tree in a green field that occupies a whole acre; it is old and highly respected by all the other trees on the hill. In its solitude it dominates the noisy stream, the hills, and the cottage across the wooden bridge. You admire it as you pass it by but on your return you look at it in a more leisurely way; its trunk is very large, deeply embedded in the earth, solid and indestructible; its branches are long, dark, and curving; it has rich shadows. In the evening it is withdrawn into itself, unapproachable, but during the daylight hours it is open and welcoming. It is whole, untouched by an axe or saw. On a sunny day you sat under it, you felt its venerable age, and because you were alone with it you were aware of the depth and the beauty of life.

At that high altitude, suddenly, very close to you was a rattler,
shrilly rattling his tail, giving a warning. You jumped.
There it was, the rattler with its triangular head, all coiled up
with its rattles in the center and its head pointed towards
you. You were a few feet away from it and it couldn't strike
you from that distance. You stared at it, and it stared back
with its unblinking eyes. You watched it for some time, its fat
suppleness, its danger; and there was no fear. Then, as you
watched, it uncoiled its head and tail towards you and moved
backwards away from you. As you moved towards it, again it
coiled, with its tail in the middle, ready to strike.
You played this game for some time until the snake got tired
and you left it and came down to the sea.

Do you think a leaf that falls to the ground is afraid of death? Do you think a bird lives in fear of dying? It meets death when death comes, but it is not concerned about death; it is much too occupied with living, with catching insects, building a nest, singing a song, flying for the very joy of flying. Have you ever watched birds soaring high up in the air without a beat of their wings, being carried along by the wind? How endlessly they seem to enjoy themselves! They are not concerned about death. If death comes, it is all right, they are finished. There is no concern about what is going to happen; they are living from moment to moment, are they not? It is we human beings who are always concerned about death—because we are not living. That is the trouble: we are dying, we are not living.

The man said a tiger had killed a buffalo the day before and would surely come back to it, and would we all, later in the evening, like to see the tiger? We said we would be delighted. He replied, "Then I will go and prepare a shelter in a tree near the carcass and tie a live goat to the tree. The tiger will first come to the live goat before going back to the old kill." We replied that we would rather not see the tiger at the expense of the goat. Presently, after some talk, he left. That evening our friend said, "Let us get into the car and go into the forest, and perhaps we may come upon that tiger." So towards sunset we drove through the forest for five or six miles and, of course, there was no tiger. Then we returned, with the headlight lighting the road. We had given up all hope of seeing the tiger and drove on without thinking about it. Just as we turned a corner—there it was, in the middle of the road, huge, its eyes bright and fixed. The car stopped, and the animal, large and threatening, came towards us, growling. It was quite close to us now, just in front of the radiator. Then it turned and came alongside the car. We put out our hand to touch it as it went by, but the friend grabbed the arm and pulled it back sharply, for he knew something of tigers. It was of great length, and as the windows were open you could smell it and its smell was not repulsive. There was a dynamic savagery about it, and great power and beauty. Still growling, it went off into the woods and we went on our way, back to the house.

A great many birds were flying overhead, some crossing the wide river and others, high up in the sky, going round in wide circles with hardly a movement of the wing. Those that were high up were mostly vultures and in the bright sun they were mere specks, tacking against the breeze. They were clumsy on land with their naked necks and wide, heavy wings. There were a few of them on the tamarind tree, and the crows were teasing them. One crow, especially, was after a vulture, trying to perch on him. The vulture got bored and took to the wing, and the crow which had been harassing him came in from behind and sat on the vulture's back as it flew. It was really quite a curious sight—the vulture with the black crow on top of it. The crow seemed to be thoroughly enjoying himself and the vulture was trying to get rid of him. Eventually, the crow flew off across the river and disappeared into the woods.

Just then, suddenly, there appeared on the window-sill a large
monkey, grey, with a black face and bushy hair over the
forehead. His hands were black and his long tail hung over
the window-sill into the room. He sat there very quiet,
almost motionless, looking at us without a movement. We
were quite close, a few feet separated us. And suddenly he
stretched out his arm, and we held hands for some time. His
hand was rough, black, and dusty, for he had climbed over
the roof, over the little parapet above the window and had
come down and sat there. He was quite relaxed, and what
was surprising was that he was extraordinarily cheerful. There
was no fear, no uneasiness; it was as though he was at home.
There he was, with the river bright golden now, and beyond
it the green bank and the distant trees. We must have held
hands for quite a time; then, almost casually, he withdrew his
hand but still remained where he was. We were looking at
each other, and you could see his black eyes shining, small
and full of strange curiosity. He wanted to come into the
room but hesitated, then stretched his arms and his legs,
reached for the parapet, and was over the roof and gone.
In the evening he was there again on a tree, high up, eating
something. We waved to him but there was no response.

It is the oldest living thing on the earth; it is gigantic in proportion, in its height and vast trunk. Among other redwood trees, which were also very old, this one was towering over them all; other trees had been touched by fire but this one had no marks on it. It had lived through all the ugly things of history, through all the wars of the world, through all the mischief and sorrow of man, through fire and lightning, through all the storms of time, untouched, majestic and utterly alone, with immense dignity.

It had been a beautiful morning, full of sunshine and shadows; the garden in the nearby hotel was full of colors—all colors— and they were so bright and the grass so green that they hurt the eye and the heart. And the mountains beyond were glistening with a freshness and a sharpness, washed by the morning dew. It was an enchanting morning and there was beauty everywhere: over the narrow bridge, across the stream, up a path into the wood, where the sunshine was playing with the leaves; they were trembling and their shadows moved. They were common plants but they outdid in their greenness and freshness all the trees that soared up to the blue skies.

At night the room was very dark and the wide window showed the whole southern sky, and into this room one night came—with a great deal of fluttering—a bird. Turning on the light and getting out of bed, one saw it under the bed. It was an owl. It was about a foot-and-a-half high with extremely wide, big eyes and a fearsome beak. We gazed at each other quite close, a few feet apart. It was frightened by the light and the closeness of a human being. We looked at each other without blinking for quite a while, and it never lost its height and its fierce dignity. You could see the cruel claws, the light feathers, and the wings tightly held against the body. One would have liked to touch it, stroke it, but it would not have allowed that. So, presently, the light was turned out and for some time there was quietness in the room. Soon there was a fluttering of the wings— you could feel the air against your face—and the owl had gone out of the window. It never came again.

As you walked on the beach the waves were enormous and they were breaking with magnificent curve and force. You walked against the wind, and suddenly you felt there was nothing between you and the sky, and this openness was heaven. To be so completely open, vulnerable—to the hills, to the sea, and to man—is the very essence of meditation.

To have no resistance, to have no barriers inwardly towards anything, to be really free, completely, from all the minor urges, compulsions, and demands, with all their little conflicts and hypocrisies, is to walk in life with open arms. And that evening, walking there on that wet sand, with the sea gulls around you, you felt the extraordinary sense of open freedom and the great beauty of love which was not in you or outside you—but everywhere.

There were a few wandering clouds in the early morning sky which was so pale, quiet, and without time. The sun was waiting for the excellency of the morning to finish. The dew was on the meadows and there were no shadows and the trees were alone, waiting for them. It was very early and even the stream was hesitant to make its boisterous run. It was quiet and the breeze hadn't yet awakened, and the leaves were still.

The moon had a halo of vaporous clouds around it;
everything was preparing to go to sleep, save the hills. They
never slept; they were always watching, waiting, looking, and
communing amongst themselves, endlessly.

The parrots and the mynas were making a great deal of noise that morning. The parrots were hardly visible among the green leaves of the trees; in the tamarind they had several holes which were their home. Their zig-zag flight was always screechy and raucous. The mynas were on the ground, fairly tame. They would let you come quite near them before they flew away. And the golden fly-catcher, the green and golden bird, was on the wires across the road. It was a beautiful morning and the sun was not too hot yet. There was a benediction in the air and there was that peace before man wakes up.

…a lily or a rose never pretends, and its beauty is that it is what it is.

There seemed to be a great rejoicing and shouting among the trees and meadows; they existed for each other and above them was heaven—not the man-made, with its tortures and hopes. And there was life, vast, splendid, throbbing, and stretching in all directions. It was life, always young and always dangerous; life that never stayed, that wandered through the earth, indifferent, never leaving a mark, never asking or calling for anything. It was there in abundance, shadowless and deathless; it didn't care from where it came or where it was going. Wherever it was there was life, beyond time and thought.

The sky is very blue, the blue that comes after the rain, and these rains have come after many months of drought. After the rain, the skies are washed clean and the hills are rejoicing, and the earth is still. And every leaf has the light of the sun on it, and the feeling of the earth is very close to you.

It has been a clear, sunny day, with long shadows and sparkling leaves; the mountains were serene, solid and close; the sky was of an extraordinary blue, spotless and gentle. Shadows filled the earth; it was a morning for shadows, the little ones and the big ones, the long lean ones and the fat satisfied ones, the squat homely one and the joyful spritely ones.

The dawn wouldn't come for a couple of hours. On waking, with eyes that have lost their sleep, one was aware of an unfathomable cheerfulness; there was no cause to it, no sentimentality or that emotional extravagance, enthusiasm, behind it; it was clear, simple cheer, uncontaminated and rich, untouched and pure. There was no thought or reason behind it and neither could one ever understand it, for there was no cause to it. This cheerfulness was pouring out of one's whole being and the being was utterly empty. As a stream of water gushes out from the side of a mountain, naturally and under pressure, this cheer was pouring out in great abundance, coming from nowhere and going nowhere, but the heart and mind would never be the same again.

At the end of every leaf, the large leaves and the tiny leaves, there was a drop of water sparkling in the sun like an extraordinary jewel. And there was a slight breeze, but that breeze didn't in any way disturb or destroy that drop on those leaves that were washed clean by the late rain. It was a very quiet morning, full of delight, peaceful, and with a sense of benediction in the air.

Do you have a sense of beauty in your life, or is it mediocre, meaningless, an everlasting struggle from morning until night? What is beauty? It isn't a sensual question, nor a sexual question. It is a very serious question because, without beauty in your heart, you cannot flower in goodness. Have you ever looked at a mountain or the blue sea without chattering, without making noise, really paying attention to the blue sea, the beauty of the water, the beauty of light on a sheet of water? When you see the extraordinary beauty of the earth, its rivers, lakes, mountains, what actually takes place? What takes place when you look at something which is actually marvelously beautiful: a statue, a poem, a lily in the pond, or a well-kept lawn? At that moment, the very majesty of a mountain makes you forget yourself. Have you ever been in that position?

If you have, you have seen that then you don't exist, only that grandeur exists. But a few seconds later or a minute later, the whole cycle begins, the confusion, the chatter. So beauty is, where you are not.

Human beings like to kill, whether it be each other, or a harmless, bright-eyed deer in the deep forest, or a tiger that has preyed upon cattle. A snake is deliberately run over on the road; a trap is set and a wolf or a coyote is caught. Well dressed, laughing people go out with their precious guns and kill birds that were lately calling to each other. A boy kills a chattering blue jay with his air gun, and the elders around him say never a word of pity, or scold him; on the contrary, they say what a good shot he is.

Sir, when you look at that mountain, if you look at it very quietly, it will tell you a lot of things; you then look more deeply, you feel the nature of it, you see the beauty of its soaring peak and curving lines. But if your mind is chattering, asking, demanding, pushing—you know all that it does—then you are not looking.

If you pass on through the meadows with their thousand flowers of every color imaginable, from bright red to yellow and purple, and their bright green grass washed clean by last night's rain, rich and verdant—again without a single movement of the machinery of thought—then you will know what love is.

With the overcrowding of cities, the noise, the exploding population, outwardly there is more and more restriction, there is less and less space. I do not know if you have noticed in this valley how new buildings are going up, there are more people, more and more cars polluting the air. Outwardly there is less and less space; if you go into any street in a crowded town you will notice this, especially in the East. In India you see thousands of people sleeping and living on the overcrowded pavement. And take any big town, London, New York, or where you will, there is hardly any space; the houses are small, people are living enclosed, trapped, and where there is no space there is violence. We have no space either ecologically, socially, or in our own mind; this is partly responsible for the violence—that we have no space.

When you look at the stars, there is you who are looking at the stars in the sky; the sky is flooded with brilliant stars, there is cool air, and there is you, the observer, the experiencer, the thinker, you with your aching heart, you, the center, creating space. You will never understand about the space between yourself and the stars, yourself and your wife or husband or friend, because you have never looked without the image, and that is why you do not know what beauty is or what love is. You talk about it, you write about it, but you have never known it except perhaps at rare intervals of total self-abandonment. So long as there is a center creating space around itself there is neither love nor beauty. When there is no center and no circumference, then there is love. And when you love you *are* beauty.

The earth was the color of the sky; the hills, the green ripening rice fields, the trees, and the dry, sandy river-bed were the color of the sky; every rock on the hills, the big boulders, were the clouds, and they were the rock. Heaven was the earth and the earth heaven; the setting sun had transformed everything. The sky was blazing fire, bursting in every streak of cloud, in every stone, in every blade of grass, in every grain of sand. The sky was ablaze with green, purple, violet, indigo, with the fury of flame.

Over that hill it was a vast sweep of purple and gold, over the southern hills a burning delicate green and fading blues; to the east there was a counter-sunset as splendid in cardinal red and burnt ochre, magenta and fading violet. The counter-sunset was exploding in splendor as in the west; a few clouds had gathered themselves around the setting sun and they were pure, smokeless fire which would never die.

The vastness of this fire and its intensity penetrated everything and entered the earth. The earth was the heavens and the heavens the earth. And everything was alive and bursting with color, and color was God, not the God of man… You were of that light, burning, furious, exploding, without shadow, without root and word. And as the sun went further down every color became more violent, more intense, and you were completely lost, past all recalling. It was an evening that had no memory.

After considering all this, is there a learning, is there an awakening of intelligence, is there a sense of order in our lives, or are we going back to the same routine? If you have that intelligence, that goodness, that sense of great love, then you will create a marvelous new society where we can all live happily. It's *our* earth—not Indian earth, or English earth, or Russian earth—it's our earth where we can live happily, intelligently, not at each other's throats. So please give your heart and mind to find out why you don't change…

Text by J. Krishnamurti drawn from books noted below. All photographs are supplied by Still Pictures archive, London

page 2
Mumbai, India—
January 1982

page 5
Introduction

page 6/7
Think on These Things

pages 8/9
On Nature and the Environment

Galen Rowell,
Peter Arnold, Inc.

pages 10/11
Krishnamurti to Himself

Mark Edwards

pages 12/13
Krishnamurti's Notebook

James L Amos,
Peter Arnold, Inc.

pages 14/15
The Only Revolution

Robert Mackinlay,
Peter Arnold, Inc.

pages 16/17
The Only Revolution

Wiggett, UNEP

pages 18/19
Krishnamurti to Himself

Peter Weiman, Bios

pages 20/21
The Only Revolution

Mark Rapillard, Bios

pages 22/23
Meeting Life

Gordon Wiltsie,
Peter Arnold, Inc.

pages 24/25
The Only Revolution

Chris Caldicott

pages 26/27
Krishnamurti's Notebook

Galen Rowell,
Peter Arnold, Inc.

pages 28/29
Krishnamurti's Journal

Ray Pfortner,
Peter Arnold, Inc.

pages 30/31
Krishnamurti to Himself

Leynar, EIA

pages 32/33
The Only Revolution

Mark Edwards

pages 34/35
Collected Works Vol. 5

Mark Edwards

pages 36/37
*Letters to the Schools,
Volume 2—
November 1983*

Mark Edwards

pages 38/39
*Letters to the Schools,
Volume 2—
November 1983*

Fritz Pölking

pages 40/41
Krishnamurti's Notebook

Petajamaki, UNEP

pages 42/43
Think on These Things

Michel Gunther, Bios

pages 44/45
Krishnamurti's Notebook

Mark Edwards

pages 46/47
The Only Revolution

Gordon Wiltsie,
Peter Arnold, Inc.

pages 48/49
Krishnamurti's Journal

Jeri Gleiter,
Peter Arnold, Inc.

pages 50/51
The Only Revolution

Wyman Meinzer,
Peter Arnold, Inc.

pages 52/53
Think on These Things

Gilles Corniere, Bios

pages 54/55
The Only Revolution

Gunter Ziesler,
Peter Arnold, Inc.

pages 56/57
The Only Revolution

Nigel J Dennis, Wildlife

pages 58/59
The Only Revolution

Ruoso Cyril, Bios

pages 60/61
Krishnamurti's Journal

John Kieffer,
Peter Arnold, Inc.

pages 62/63
Krishnamurti's Notebook

Jean-Louis Le Moigne,
Bios

pages 64/65
The Only Revolution

Kim Heacox,
Peter Arnold, Inc.

pages 66/67
Meditations

FOTO-UNEP

pages 68/69
Krishnamurti's Notebook

Clyde H Smith,
Peter Arnold, Inc.

pages 70/71
Krishnamurti's Notebook

Werner H Muller,
Peter Arnold, Inc.

pages 72/73
The Only Revolution

Kevin Schafer,
Peter Arnold, Inc.

pages 74/75
Think on These Things

Mark Edwards

pages 76/77
Krishnamurti's Notebook

Jean-Claude Bacle, Bios

pages 78/79
Meditations

Werner H Muller,
Peter Arnold, Inc.

pages 80/81
Krishnamurti's Notebook

Jeri Gleiter,
Peter Arnold, Inc.

pages 82/83
Krishnamurti's Notebook

Martin Hawes

pages 84/85
Krishnamurti to Himself

J Frebet, Bios

pages 86/87
Mumbai, India—
January 1982

Friedrich Grohe

pages 88/89
*Commentaries on
Living, Second Series*

Mark Edwards

pages 90/91
Collected Works Vol. 15

Friedrich Grohe

pages 92/93
The Only Revolution

Clyde H Smith,
Peter Arnold, Inc.

pages 94/95
*The Awakening of
Intelligence*

Mark Edwards

pages 96/97
*Freedom from the
Known*

Vincent Decorde, Bios

pages 98/99
Krishnamurti's Notebook

Jim Wark, Peter Arnold

pages 100/101
Krishnamurti's Notebook

Johnson, UNEP

pages 102/103
Krishnamurti's Notebook

Keith Kent,
Peter Arnold, Inc.

page 105
Chennai, India—
December 1979

Evelyne Blau has been a trustee of the Krishnamurti Foundation of America since 1973. She is the producer of two feature-length documentary films on Krishnamurti, *The Challenge of Change* and *With a Silent Mind,* as well as a television series *Beyond Myth and Tradition.* Her centennial book *Krishnamurti 100 Years* presents Krishnamurti's life as seen through the eyes of witnesses over the period of a century.

Mark Edwards first met Krishnamurti in 1968 in order to photograph him. This meeting sparked a passionate desire to photograph environmental problems around the world. Since then he has worked on assignments in over 100 countries and founded *Still Pictures,* the photo library specializing in environmental issues and nature. He continued to photograph Krishnamurti for various publications throughout his life. In 1991 he worked with Professor David Bohm on *Changing Consciousness,* published by Harper Collins.